WHAT GOES ON INSIDE YOUR BRAIN?

LEFT BRAIN VS. RIGHT BRAIN

JAMES BOW

Gareth Stevens PUBLISHING

Please visit our website, www.garethstevens.com.
For a free color catalog of all our high-quality books,
call toll free 1-800-542-2595 or fax 1-877-542-2596.

Cataloging-in-Publication Data
Names: Bow, James.
Title: Left brain vs. right brain / James Bow.
Description: New York : Gareth Stevens Publishing, 2019. | Series: What goes on inside your brain? | Includes glossary and index.
Identifiers: ISBN 9781538235669 (pbk.) | ISBN 9781538235676 (library bound)
Subjects: LCSH: Cerebral dominance--Juvenile literature. | Brain--Localization of functions--Juvenile literature. | Brain--Juvenile literature.
Classification: LCC QP385.5 B68 2019 | DDC 612.8'25--dc23

First Edition

Published in 2019 by
Gareth Stevens Publishing
111 East 14th Street, Suite 349
New York, NY 10003

Produced by Calcium
Editors: Sarah Eason and Claudia Martin
Designers: Paul Myerscough and Jeni Child

Photo credits: Cover: Shutterstock/Lev Malevich. Inside: Shutterstock: Alexander Raths: p.42; Alex Brylov: p.21; casey christopher: p.36; cheapbooks: p.17; cloki: p.18; Concept Photo: p.20; Cyrsiam: p.19; Dan Kosmayer: p.15; decade3D/anatomy online: p.8; DGLimages: p.43; Dim Dimich p.5; Dragon Images: p.16; Gena Melendrez: p.35; goodluz: p.13; grafvision: p.1; GWImages: p.24; JumlongCH: p.28; Kaesler Media: p.40; Karuka: p.26; Kirasolly: p.27; Mary A Lupo: p.9; MriMan: p.32; Monkey Business Images: p.44; Nerthuz: p.4; Pand P Studio: p.37; Paranamir: p.38; pathdoc: p.30; Pavel Krasensky: p.34; Potato Tomato: p.11; Puwadol Jaturawutthichai: p.14; Rawpixel.com: p.41; sirtravelalot: p.31; Samuel Borges Photography: p.1, p.22; Sanja Karin Music: p.29; sfam photo: p.6, p.25; Sokolova Maryna: p.12; stockfour: p.10; Tatiana Shepeleva: p.45; Tefi: p.39; Tuzemka: p.33; VILevi: p.23; vystekimages: p.7.

Printed in the United States of America

CPSIA compliance information: Batch #CW19GS
For further information contact Gareth Stevens, New York, New York at 1-800-542-2595.

CONTENTS

CHAPTER 1

THE HUMAN BRAIN

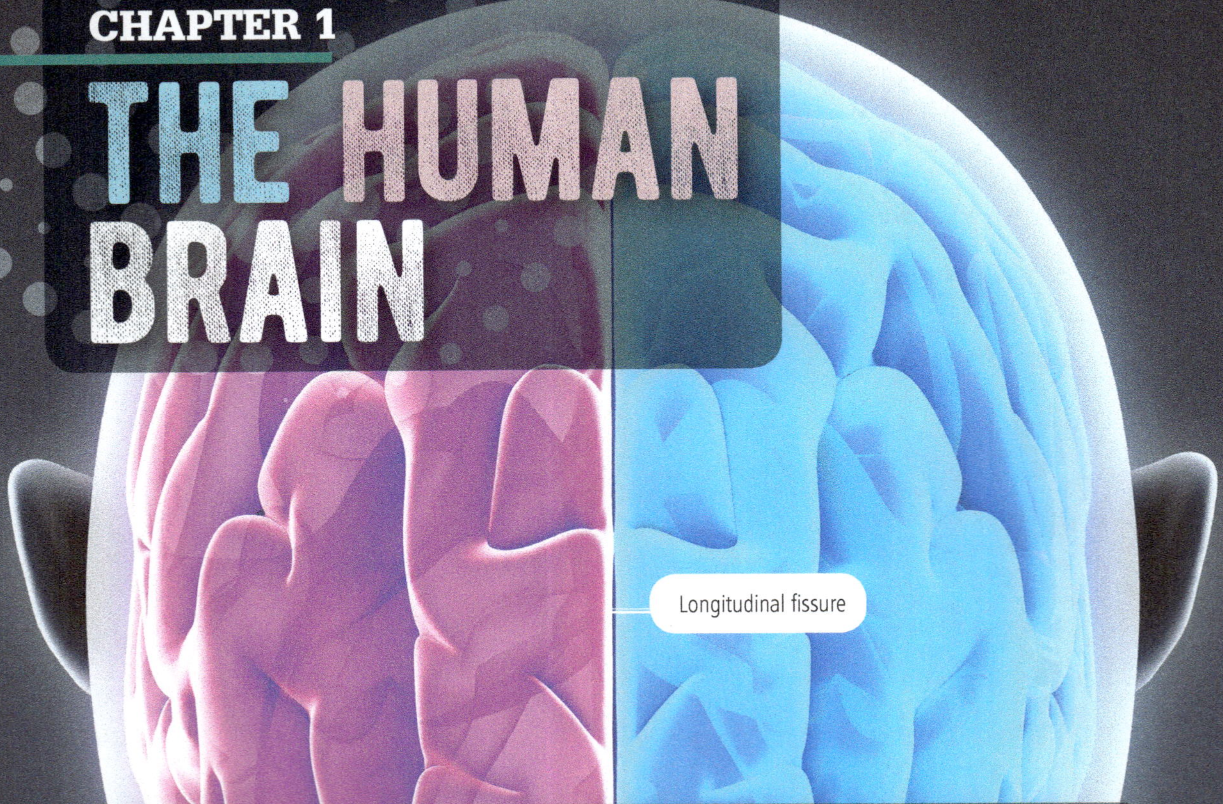

You may not realize the many ways you are using your brain right now. Thanks to your brain, you are reading these words. Your brain helped you get up this morning, meet friends, and wonder about the mysteries of the universe. And one of the biggest of all mysteries is the brain itself!

Your brain is the most complex organ in your body. It is about as large as two fists. Beneath its wrinkled surface are more than 100 billion nerve cells, called neurons, communicating with one another through trillions of connections called synapses. The brain has three main parts: the brain stem, cerebellum, and cerebrum.

The gap that divides the left hemisphere from the right hemisphere of your brain is called the longitudinal fissure or cerebral fissure.

The brain stem handles automatic functions like your heartbeat and breathing. It is the oldest part of the brain in terms of evolution. It is also found in most other animals, including reptiles and birds.

The cerebellum, at the rear of the brain, has been linked to muscle control, movement, and balance. Finally, there is the cerebrum, the largest part of the human brain. Its outer layer is called the cerebral cortex—most of the things brains do that make us human, such as thought and conscious action, are found here.

Two Hemispheres

The brain has a deep cut through the middle of the cerebrum, splitting it into left and right sides, or hemispheres. The jobs the cerebrum and the cerebral cortex do are divided between the two hemispheres. Most animal brains are divided into hemispheres. Humans and other mammals have the most developed hemispheres. The human hemispheres make up two-thirds of the whole brain. Like humans, other animals show signs of their different hemispheres controlling different things.

INSIDE YOUR BRAIN

Scientists who study the brain, called neurologists, divide each hemisphere of the cerebral cortex into four parts, called lobes. There is plenty of crossover between where different processes happen, but the frontal lobe is very active in reasoning and planning. The parietal lobe is linked with processing sensory information. The occipital lobe is linked with vision. The temporal lobe is linked with memory, recognition of sounds, and speech.

The cerebral cortex is divided into four lobes. The brain stem connects the brain to the spinal cord.

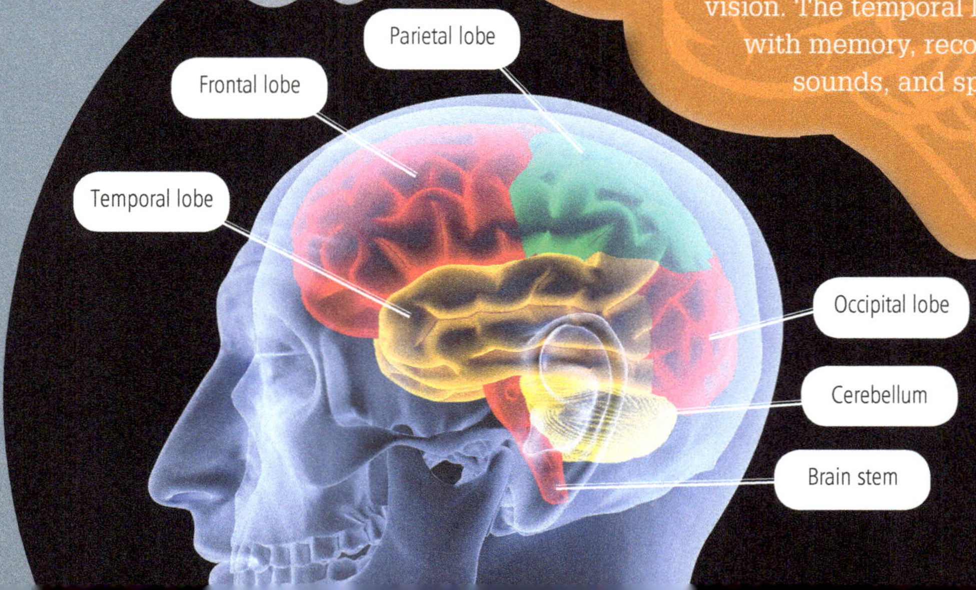

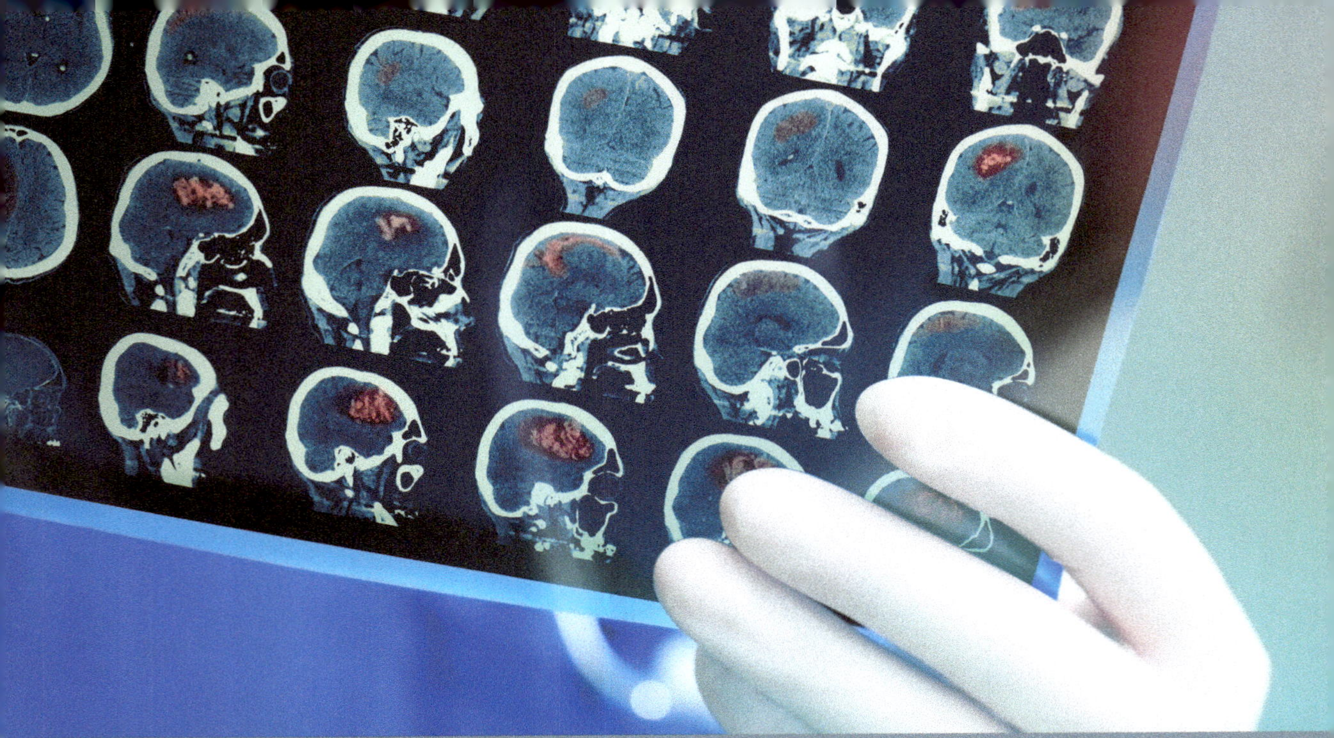

Myths About Left and Right

Brain mapping took a big step in the 1970s, when positron emission tomography showed which parts of the brain were used during certain activities.

You may have heard about your "left brain" and "right brain." People commonly believe that the two parts of the brain have separate functions. You may have heard that "left-brained" people are good at mathematics, science, and logical reasoning, and that the left side of the brain is where rational thought takes place. "Right-brained" people are commonly believed to be more emotional, or better at understanding emotions, and to be more artistic, creative, or imaginative. This is a myth. Neurologists know that when it comes to doing mathematics, using language, or composing music, both sides of the brain are used.

The Reality

Doctors, including neurologists, have been studying the brain for centuries. In the past few decades, new technologies have allowed us to see activity inside the brain. For example, positron emission tomography (PET) scans measure levels of the sugar glucose in the brain to show where the brain's neurons are active. This works because active neurons use glucose as fuel. Thanks to such techniques, we have begun to build up a picture of which parts of the brain are used when we are carrying out different activities.

What we now know is that the left and right sides of our brains do actually do different things. The difference in the functions of the left and right hemispheres of the brain is called lateralization. The left hemisphere controls the muscles of the right side of the body, and the right hemisphere controls the left side of the body. The left hemisphere is usually used when a person speaks. In addition, understanding the meaning of words and the way they are put together activates portions of the left side of the brain. For some activities, one side of the brain seems to dominate over the other. Research suggests that over 88 percent of people tend to use their right hand rather than their left for writing or other tasks. Many of these people also favor listening through their right ear.

During most activities, however, both sides of the brain work together as partners. The right hemisphere, for example, listens to how words sound, and can decide whether a person is speaking honestly or deceptively. While the left brain can do calculations, the right brain helps with estimating and comparing results.

SPEAK YOUR MIND

How well do you write with each hand? Do you turn a particular ear toward a sound when you want to listen closely? How do you think the fact that most people are right-handed changes how tools are made? Give reasons for your answers.

Most scissors are designed for use by right-handed people, with the right blade on top.

Linking the Halves Together

The left and right hemispheres of the human brain are joined by a bundle of nerves called the corpus callosum. This link is found below the cerebral cortex, linking the two sides of the cerebrum together. In most humans, the link is 4 inches (10 cm) long. It contains 200–250 million nerve cells called axons. At either end of the corpus callosum, these axons radiate out, passing into the cerebral cortex. Signals between the two hemispheres pass through this link. The corpus callosum is found only in mammals that are not marsupials. For other animals, different structures are used to connect the hemispheres together.

The corpus callosum makes up the majority of the brain's "white matter." White matter is mainly nerve fibers, which transmit signals from neurons, which make up the "gray matter" of the brain.

The corpus callosum shows us how constantly the two sides of the brain work together. We need a very thick cable of brain cells to pass an endless stream of signals between the two hemispheres.

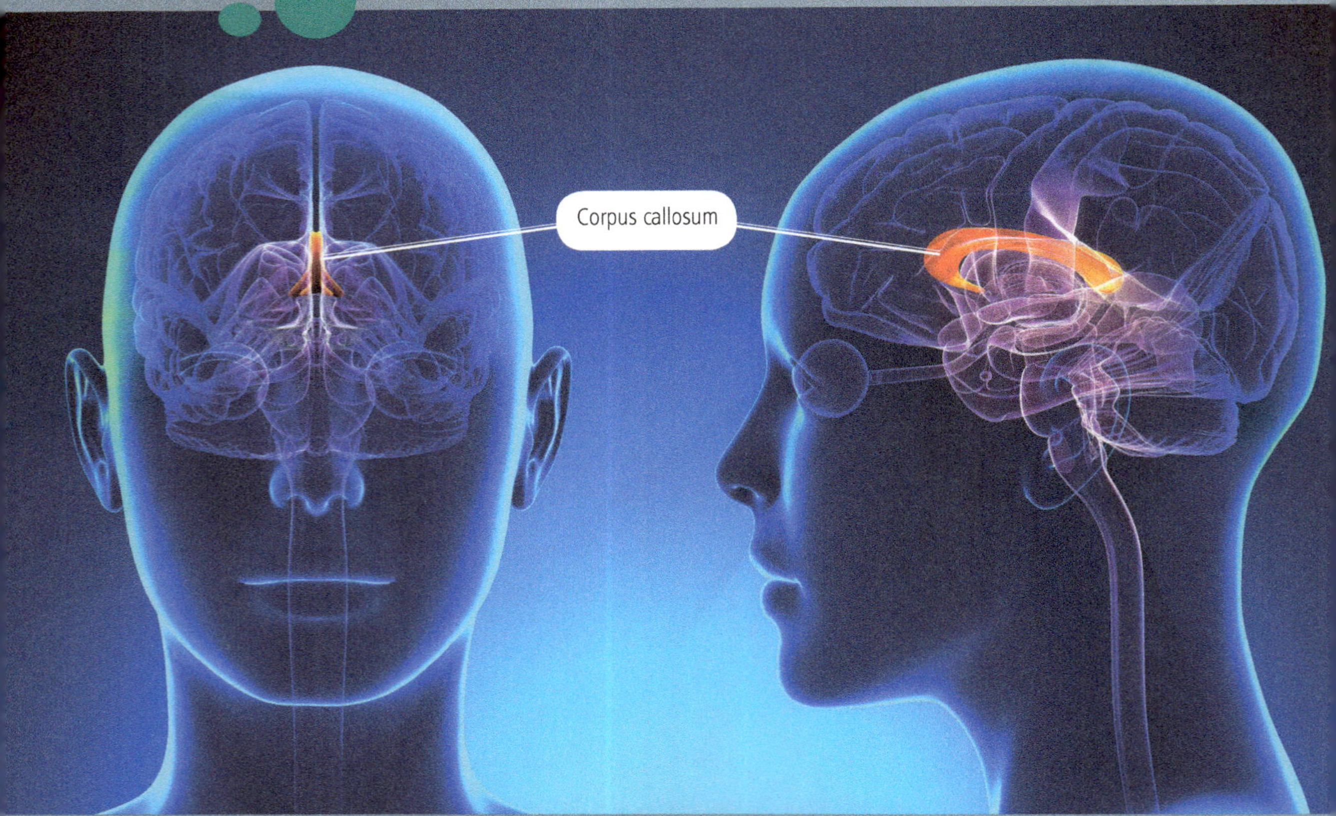

Randy Johnson was a left-handed major league baseball pitcher. Left-handed pitchers are prized as they are harder for right-handed batters to hit.

Its thickness also reveals how busy and well-developed each side of the brain is independently.

Lopsided Brain

Our brains are asymmetrical, even though our skulls are symmetrical. The left hemisphere is larger at the back (posterior), and the right hemisphere is larger at the front (anterior). We know that each lobe of the brain does different things, so the fact that the hemispheres have grown differently suggests that each hemisphere of the brain has adapted to favor certain functions.

Although we know more than we did 100 years ago, there are still plenty of questions about how the brain functions, why it is divided the way it is, and how the different parts, including the two hemispheres, work together.

SPEAK YOUR MIND

The world seems to be dominated by people who are right-handed. The dominance of the right hand shows up in language itself. The English word "left" comes from the Anglo-Saxon word "*lyft*," meaning weak. The Latin word for left is "*sinistra*," which has become the English word "sinister." In Hindi, the left hand is called the "*ulta haanth*," which translates as "wrong hand." It was not long ago that left-handed people were discouraged from favoring their left hands and forced to write with their right. How do you think that made them feel? Do you think it helped them learn? Give reasons for your answers.

CHAPTER 2

THE LEFT BRAIN

Math is thought of as a left-brain activity, but the left side gets help from the right in figuring out math problems.

The popular concept of the left hemisphere is that it is where logical thinking takes place, and where language is stored. It has sometimes been called "the digital brain" and compared to a computer. It is true that the left side of the brain is used when people perform step-by-step instructions, and when a person hears words and understands them or speaks up. However, this only scratches the surface of what the left hemisphere does.

We know that the two hemispheres of the brain make up the cerebrum and cerebral cortex. We know that each hemisphere has four lobes: the frontal, parietal, occipital, and temporal. The frontal lobes are linked to reasoning and planning, solving problems, and reacting emotionally. The parietal lobes handle movement, recognize objects, and respond to much information from the senses, such as touch, temperature, and pain. The occipital lobes handle what the brain sees through the eyes, while the temporal lobes process signals about sounds from the ears, and are linked with storing many of the brain's memories. Although the four sets of paired lobes are almost mirror images of one another, the left and right hemispheres divide the functions of the brain in a different way.

SPEAK YOUR MIND

Do you prefer doing math or creative writing? How is the process of solving math problems different from the process of writing stories? What would the benefits be of a brain that could only solve math or logic problems? What would be the drawbacks? Give reasons for your answers.

Seeing a Bicycle

Let us imagine that a person looks at a bicycle. Both eyes send signals to both hemispheres. These signals travel first to the occipital lobes, but then the other lobes get involved to process and respond to the information in countless different ways. If we mapped the complex pathways between the lobes, they would look different on each side of the brain. When the image of the bicycle is seen by the right brain, it may generate an emotion of happiness (involving the frontal lobe) as the person imagines riding on it. The left side of the brain sees the bicycle and knows that it is named a bicycle (involving the parietal lobe). The left side of the brain knows how to get on the bike and ride it (involving several lobes, including the temporal). The lobes of each hemisphere are working together in response to seeing the bike, yet the hemispheres are dealing with that information differently.

Both hemispheres of the brain rely on the cerebellum's sense of balance and coordination in order to ride the bike.

Right-Handedness

One thing the left side of the brain has almost total control over is the right half of the body. Parts of the left brain are used when a person moves muscles on their right side, writes with their right hand, or listens with their right ear. Hand preference develops young. One scientific study in 2013 showed that at 14 months old, only 39 percent of infants favored using one hand over the other to grip objects. Meanwhile, by 24 months, 97 percent of toddlers had a preference.

Why would our brains favor using one side of the body over the other? There are many theories about this lateralization. One theory is that the brain is simply dividing up work between the two hemispheres as it is more efficient if one side of the brain does certain jobs rather than both. Speech is mostly controlled by the left side of the brain and, since speech is so important to humans, this may explain why so much of our population is "left-dominant," or right-handed. However, this theory suggests that for left-handed people, the division of labor in the brain should be reversed, with more activities controlled by the right brain. While left-handers do use parts of their right hemispheres more often than right-handers, not all brain activity in a left-handed person is the mirror image of all brain activity in a right-handed person.

Although it is a little early to say, this baby may already be showing a preference for his right hand, which means that his left brain will be dominant while using a pen.

All these students are writing with their right hands, although—particularly if they are doing creative writing—they may heavily be using their right brains to imagine a story.

Runs in the Family

There is another theory that handedness is genetic. If both your parents are left-handed, you have a 26 percent chance of being left-handed. If neither of your parents is left-handed, you have a less than 10 percent chance. However, scientists have not been able to find a single gene that determines if you are right- or left-handed. If this theory is correct, it is likely that handedness is controlled by a range of genes working together.

INSIDE YOUR BRAIN

A dominant hand does not mean one entire hemisphere of the brain is dominant in all activities and thought processes. Doctors did magnetic resonance imaging (MRI) and PET scans of over 1,000 patients and found no sign that most people were favoring one side of the brain over the other in a range of activities. This is because the hemispheres of the brain always work together.

Damage on the Left

One way to understand how a brain works is to see what happens when it is damaged. Neurologists are particularly interested in seeing how the brain's activity changes after trauma. This can happen in a number of ways, from a fall or car accident to a medical problem like a stroke. The brain shows impressive resilience and adaptability when recovering from injury.

Since the left hemisphere of the brain has been linked to thinking through things in order, and understanding and using words, damage to the left side of the brain affects these abilities. People with left-brain injury may have trouble finding the right word or understanding what is said to them. Although the other side of the brain is sometimes able to step in, patients lose some control over the right side of the body.

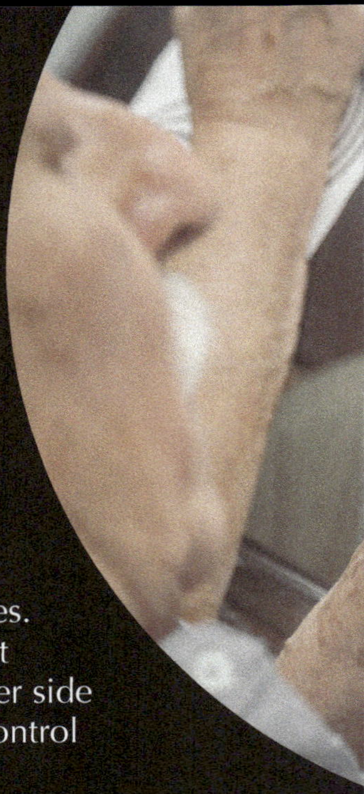

An MRI scan highlights the damage done to the brain of a patient. In the United States alone, more than 2 million people suffer brain injuries every year.

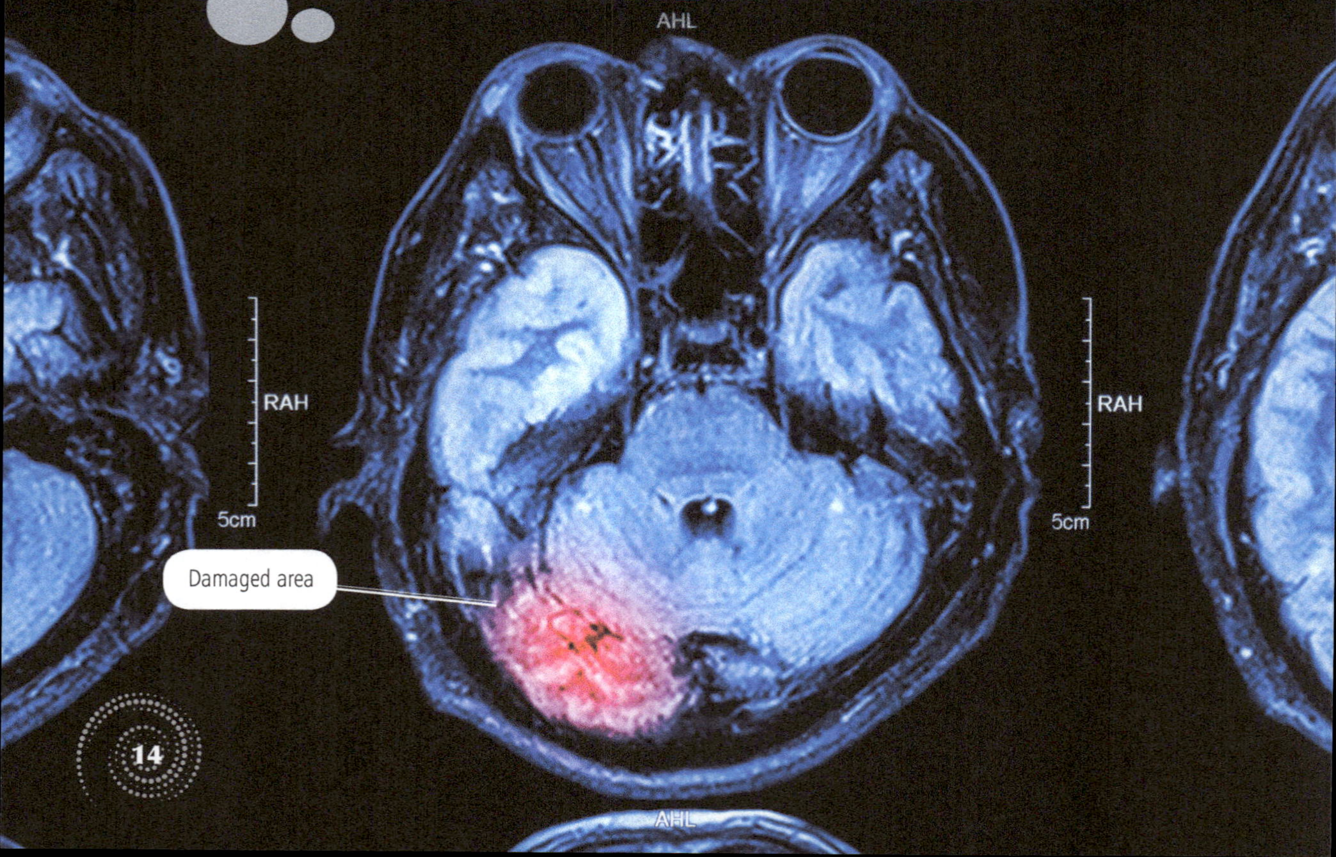

People suffering from damage to the left side of the brain may take rehabilitation classes that help them with logical thinking and use of the right side of their body.

In some cases, people suffering damage to the left side of their brain found they had trouble paying attention. Although people with damage to their left hemispheres could look at a picture and understand the whole of it, they found it hard to identify the individual details of the picture, which suggests that the left side of the brain provides focus and close attention.

Recovering and Changing

Patients can recover from traumatic brain injuries. Even a fully mature brain has neuroplasticity, which means the ability to change throughout a person's life. The brain does not heal as fast as other parts of the body, but the cells of the brain can change, and new synapses, or connections, can be formed. Functions that were performed in a damaged part of a brain can be moved to other parts of the brain through training and therapy. This suggests that the division of the hemispheres is less important to the functions of the brain than many think.

SPEAK YOUR MIND

A hemispherectomy is a rarely done surgery in which an entire hemisphere of the brain is removed. This operation was first attempted in 1928, and on severely epileptic patients in the 1960s. While removing the left hemisphere did cause some loss of language, the younger the patient was, the better the remaining brain was able to adapt. One patient who went through the surgery at age five went on to attend college and get above average grades. Why would young people be better able to recover from brain damage than older people? Give reasons for your answer.

CHAPTER 3

THE RIGHT BRAIN

The right hemisphere has been linked to emotional reactions, intuition, imagination, musical ability, and artistic skills. It is said to not focus on small details or facts, but instead to respond more broadly to the wider world. For this reason, the right side of the brain has been called "the creative brain." Is all of this true?

This painter may be using her right brain to creatively compose her picture, but she is using her right hand to paint.

The right side of the brain controls the left side of the body. People who are left-handed are said to have a right-dominant brain. However, people who are left-handed are not using their right hemispheres a great deal more than their left, because both hemispheres cooperate constantly. For example, a person may use a tool with their left hand, using the right hemisphere to control their muscles in that hand. However, the information about the tool and how to use it remains stored in the left hemisphere of the brain.

Painting a Picture

The right brain is good at recognizing faces and reading emotions. It helps the left's speech centers by hearing the tone of how words are spoken and understanding things like context and metaphor (a figure of speech that is not meant to be taken literally). The right brain is used heavily when we are processing visual information and understanding the space around us. While the left hemisphere is often used when adding, subtracting, multiplying, or dividing numbers, the right hemisphere has math skills, too. It is often used to estimate the size or value of things or to compare one thing against another. During many activities, it appears that the right side of the brain looks at the world differently from the left side of the brain, but in a way that adds to what the left side can do, for the benefit of the person as a whole.

SPEAK YOUR MIND

The right brain is linked with emotional reactions, while the left is linked to logic. When was the last time you reacted to something with strong emotion? Was your reaction the right one? What would you do differently if you could live through that moment again? Would applying more logical thought have helped? Give reasons for your answers.

The right hemisphere focuses on how an emotion feels, while the left hemisphere labels the emotions expressed.

Dark Thoughts

The right hemisphere is often characterized as more emotional than the left hemisphere, and it has also been linked to depression. Depression is not a simple emotion, but a series of negative emotions and pessimistic thoughts. Unusual activity in the right brain has been observed in people dealing with depression, and it may be caused by the right hemisphere's tendency to second-guess decisions made by the left hemisphere.

This is not the same thing as saying that those who are left-handed are more likely to be depressed. The brain is far too complicated to draw this conclusion. However, depression does hint at the right hemisphere's role of being on alert. The right brain looks out for threats. It plays "devil's advocate" when a person makes a decision. As a defense mechanism, it looks at all of the things that could go wrong.

Overactive Right Hemisphere

If the right hemisphere of the brain is too active, it can lead to us always second-guessing ourselves, and always thinking that the worst will happen. And because the left hemisphere is often associated with making decisions and processing happy experiences, a lack of use of the left hemisphere compared to the right could lead to long-term feelings of sadness. It could also lead to being unable to make decisions—something that is often associated with depression.

A strange fact is that the right frontal lobe is more active when people are feeling sad, but the left frontal lobe is more active when people are happy. Learning what calms the right frontal lobe could help people reduce sadness.

An overactive right hemisphere can also affect the body physically. It has been associated with a condition called hypercortisolemia, where the hormone cortisol is released into the body. Cortisol is a stress hormone that increases heart rate, blood pressure, and blood sugar while tensing up muscles and shutting down nonessential body functions. It is useful in small bursts when you have to run from danger, but if cortisol is pushed through your body for long periods, it harms your immune system and makes it easier for you to get sick. Frequent illness is a common characteristic of depressed patients. All of this demonstrates how important it is for the two hemispheres of the brain to work together in balance.

SPEAK YOUR MIND

How often do you second-guess your decisions? How often do you worry about your future? Are your concerns reasonable or based on emotion? Why could it be important for your brain to question its own decisions? Give reasons for your answers.

Cortisol helps the fight or flight response, which is a way the brain gets the body to respond to an immediate danger.

Damage on the Right

Brain damage to the right hemisphere is just as traumatic as to the left, but patients sometimes react differently to these injuries. As we have seen, the right hemisphere often acts as a soldier on alert. It is always looking at the wider world and responding to external stimuli.

People who lose their right hemispheres, due to injury or other medical problems, experience a narrowing of their window of attention, sometimes to the point where they fail to acknowledge the existence of the left half of their body. They can leave food untouched on the left side of their plate. The right hemisphere of the brain is able to understand metaphor, implied rather than stated meaning, context, and body language. Damage to this hemisphere sometimes causes these skills to disappear. Patients can lose the ability to understand humor or jokes. They understand words literally and no longer understand if a word is being used in a different context, as a symbol of something else. A patient can look at a picture and not understand what it is about, even though they can identify individual details.

Researchers at Harvard University suggest that 2 out of every 100 people have trouble recognizing faces. In our complex society, this can be tricky!

Teachers who suffer from face blindness may memorize the seating arrangements to help them recognize their students.

Face Blindness

One condition that can result from damage to the right hemisphere is prosopagnosia, or "face blindness." This is a medical condition where the portion of the right hemisphere controlling facial recognition is damaged or underdeveloped. Such patients are otherwise normal in their thinking, but they cannot recognize people's faces. A related medical issue is called the "Capgras delusion." Here, the patient recognizes the face, but the part of the brain that remembers what the face means to the patient is damaged, so the patient does not have the normal reaction to seeing someone they recognize, like a loved one. This conflict can lead them to believe that their friends or loved ones have been replaced by identical imposters.

INSIDE YOUR BRAIN

Do you have trouble recognizing people when you bump into them in unexpected places? Studies suggest that 2.5 percent of the population has some form of face blindness. People with mild cases can get better through specialist training. Others use clues to identify people they need to know. For example, teachers may focus on clues like the backpacks students bring to school.

CHAPTER 4

EXPLORING THE HEMISPHERES

The brain was an almost complete mystery until very recently. The seventeenth-century English doctor Thomas Willis was one of the first to study the physical brain in detail. He wrote about its structure and identified the brain stem, cerebellum, and hemispheres. However, he had no idea how the brain actually worked. The discovery that handedness was connected to the brain was not made until centuries later.

Thanks to doctors like Paul Broca, we know that the front left of the brain is used for speaking, while the back left is used for understanding speech.

The first discoveries about lateralization (the different functions of the two hemispheres) came in the mid-nineteenth century, from doctors studying brain-damaged patients. French doctor Paul Broca studied a patient nicknamed "Tan." Tan had aphasia, which meant he had great difficulty speaking. "Tan" was one of the only words he could say. After Tan died, Broca did an autopsy on Tan's brain, and noticed there was a lesion, or cut, in Tan's left frontal lobe. This led to the conclusion that this part of the brain was responsible for some aspects of speech.

Other doctors followed a similar path, tracing problems to damage in specific parts of the brain. German physician Karl Wernicke found that damage to the back left of the brain made it harder for people to understand words, rather than speak them. Gradually, the functions of the brain started to be mapped out.

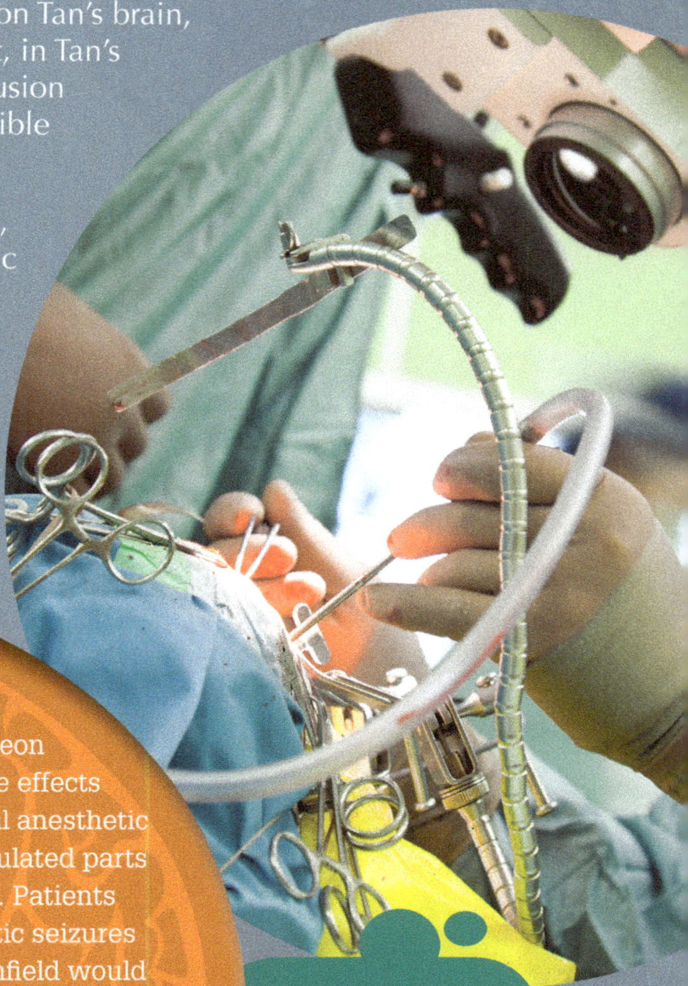

The work of Wilder Penfield helped doctors and surgeons better understand the brain, and also proved that one hemisphere's cortex controls the muscles of the opposite side of the body.

INSIDE YOUR BRAIN

In the 1940s, Canadian neurosurgeon Wilder Penfield tried to reduce the side effects of surgery to cure epilepsy. He used a local anesthetic so the patient remained awake, then stimulated parts of their brain with small electric shocks. Patients had previously reported that their epileptic seizures started with a smell like burned toast. Penfield would stimulate different spots in the brain until the patient reported smelling burned toast. Then Penfield knew he had found his target and was able to operate just on that small area of the brain.

Split Brain Operations

Starting in the late 1950s, neurosurgeons and neurologists went through a period of cutting into the brains of patients in quite a drastic manner. To treat severe epileptic seizures, one method was to cut the corpus callosum. As we have learned, this is the bundle of nerves that connects the left and right hemispheres of the brain—it also allows seizure impulses to spread from one side of the brain to the other. Patients who underwent the procedure, which was only carried out as a last resort, were closely studied by doctors like Michael Gazzaniga and Roger Sperry to see how their brains changed when the two hemispheres were separated from each other.

Alien Hand

A patient known as Vicki was one of the patients to undergo this surgery. She described her first months after the surgery as "infuriating." She would

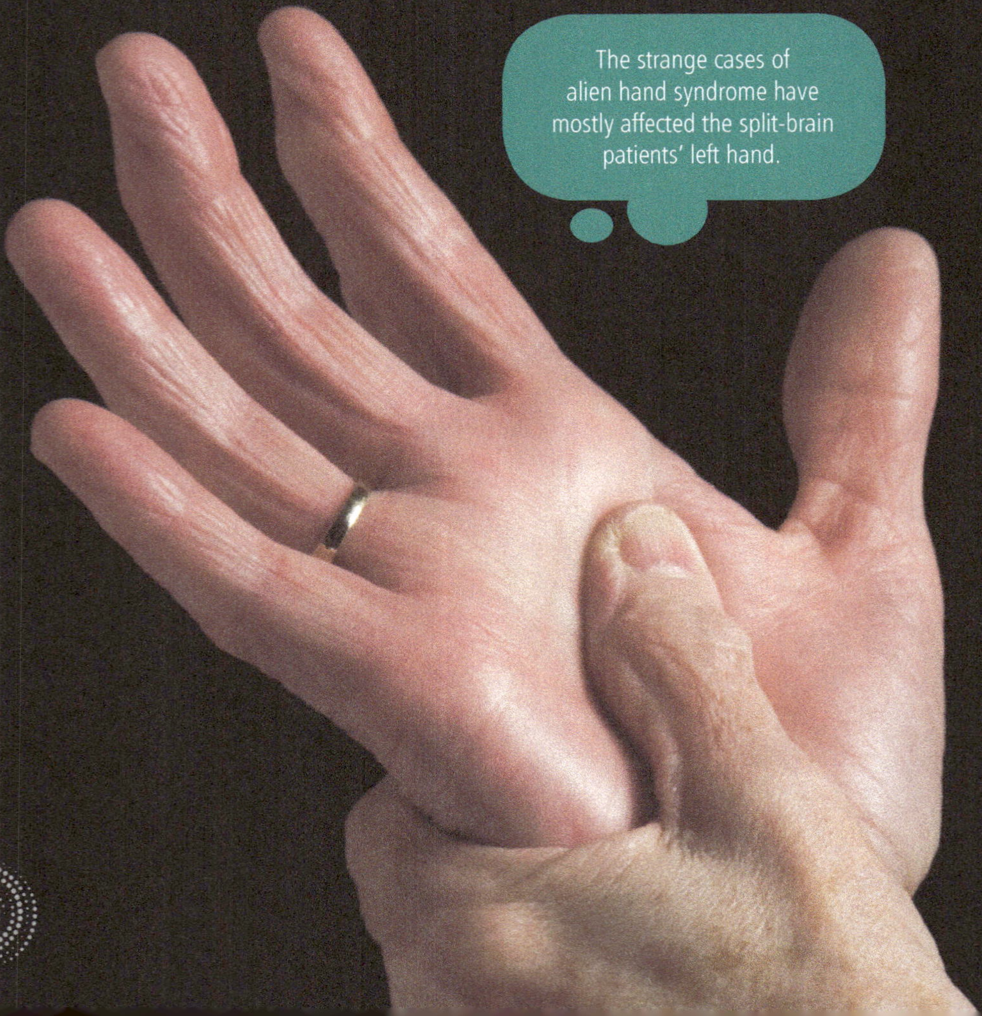

The strange cases of alien hand syndrome have mostly affected the split-brain patients' left hand.

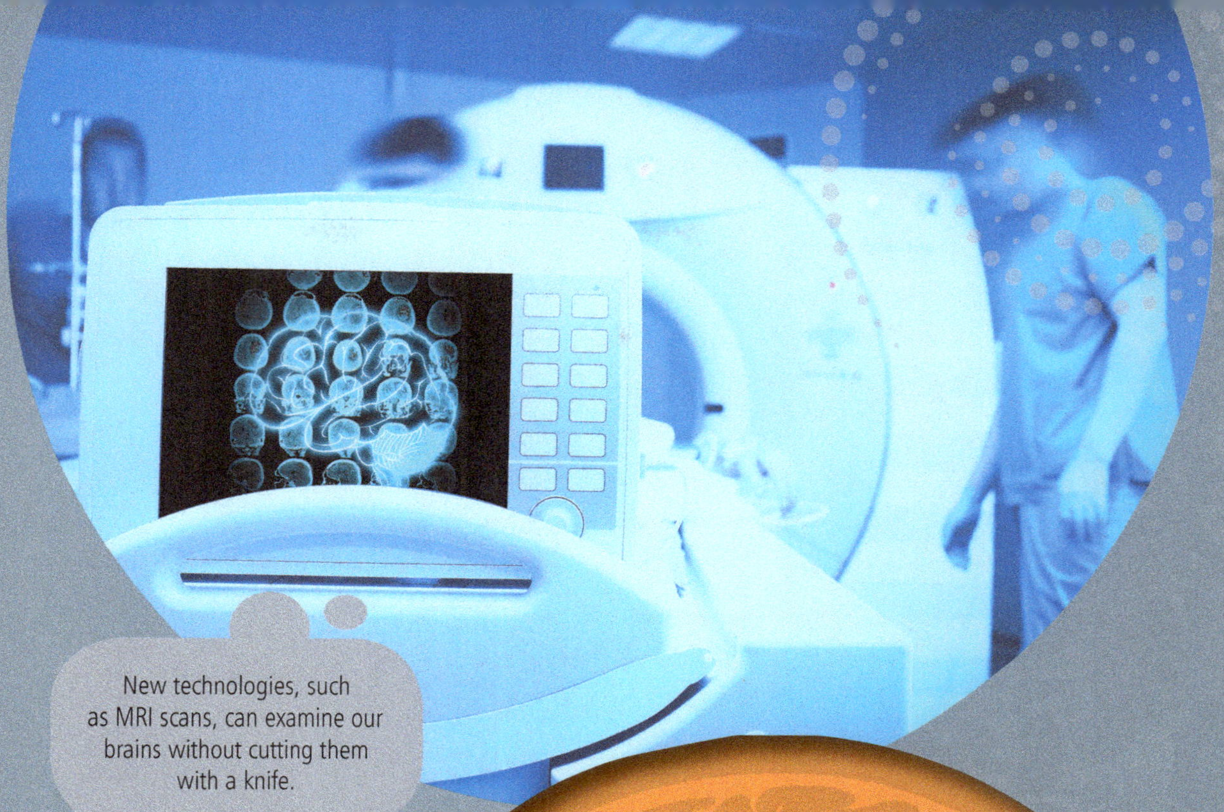

New technologies, such as MRI scans, can examine our brains without cutting them with a knife.

go grocery shopping, see something she wanted on the shelf, and reach out with her right hand, only to have her left come in and interfere. This is called "alien hand syndrome." Her hands not only had difficulty coordinating, but they disagreed on what she should pick up! After about a year, Vicki's difficulties improved.

Vicki was not alone. A number of patients who had gone through the surgery, and others who had their corpus callosum damaged, found half of their body acting independently of the other half. One patient's left hand acted aggressively, striking out at his wife for no reason. The patient's right hand had to grab his left to stop it.

INSIDE YOUR BRAIN

An MRI scanner is good for finding problems like brain tumors. Most of the body is made of water molecules, which consist of hydrogen and oxygen atoms. At the center of a hydrogen atom is a particle called a proton. Protons are like tiny magnets. Magnets in an MRI scanner turn all the protons to face one way. Radio waves then knock the protons out of alignment. When the radio waves are turned off, the protons realign. This sends out radio signals, which are used to build a three-dimensional (3D) picture.

In Two Minds

Another patient, referred to as WJ, also had his corpus callosum cut. Doctors tested his ability to do mathematics by showing simple questions on one side of his field of vision or the other. Although both our eyes send messages to both hemispheres, the left side of our field of vision is processed by the right hemisphere and vice versa. The left hemisphere was able to answer the questions correctly 90 percent of the time, while the right hemisphere only got the right answers by chance. Doctors also tested WJ's ability to recognize familiar faces. Again, they did this by flashing pictures of familiar faces on one side or the other. This showed that the right hemisphere was way better at recognizing faces than the left.

Another test carried out on patients with split brains is to flash up a word so it can be seen in only the left or right side of the field of vision. The patient is then told to repeat what they saw. If a word like "elephant" is flashed on the right side of the screen, it is registered by the left hemisphere of the brain, and the patient calls out that they see the word "elephant." However, if the word is flashed on the left side of the screen, the patient may say that they do not see anything. However, their left hand may draw a picture of an elephant, often to the surprise of the patient.

Some split-brained patients can draw an object with their left hand if the word has been shown in their left field of vision, even if they do not consciously know what the word was.

This widely believed idea of the rational left brain and emotional, creative right brain is too simplified, but it was sparked by cases of split-brained patients like Paul S.

Two Answers

In another case, a boy with a split brain, referred to as "Paul S," was asked the same question, first in one ear, then the other. This allowed researchers to question both hemispheres, which answered questions differently. Asked what he wanted to be when he grew up, the right side of Paul's brain answered, "An automobile racer," while the left replied, "A draftsman" (a person who makes detailed plans for building things). Cases like this helped spark the theory that the right hemisphere of the brain was more emotional, and the left side of the brain more rational.

SPEAK YOUR MIND

What would you like to be when you grow up? Think about your answer. Are you responding emotionally or rationally? If you think about your answer some more, is it likely to change? Do you feel that different parts of your brain are arguing over your decision? Give reasons for your answers.

Rain Man

Perhaps the most famous split-brained individual was Kim Peek. His life was the inspiration for the Oscar-winning 1988 movie *Rain Man*, starring Dustin Hoffman and Tom Cruise. Kim did not have surgery to cut his corpus callosum. Instead, he was born with a malformed cerebellum and no corpus callosum.

The problems with Kim's brain meant he was not able to do everyday tasks like button up his shirt. However, he made up for this in other ways. He was able to memorize over 9,000 books. He stored encyclopedia-levels of information on subjects like history, sports, movies, and directions to get to any major U.S. city. Because of this, he was called a "savant," or someone who has certain abilities far exceeding the average. Although scientists do not believe these skills were connected to his lack of a corpus callosum, the split in his hemispheres explained why he was able to read books so quickly. He could split his vision and read two separate pages at once! He also had well-developed language centers in both hemispheres of the brain, rather than in just the left temporal lobe, so he could use and communicate that information.

Kim Peek's skills, and the movie about him, made Peek a celebrity. Because Peek did not go through a split-brain surgery, he is seen as a natural example of what happens if the two hemispheres of the brain are split from each other. In 2004, he helped scientists scan his brain to produce a 3D map of his brain's structure and how it worked. His case helped neurologists better understand what the corpus callosum does and how the two sides of our brain communicate.

Your neurons are firing small amounts of electricity to send their signals. This electricity can be detected by magnets.

INSIDE YOUR BRAIN

A magnetoencephalography (MEG) scanner measures the electrical currents that pass through your brain as the nerves send signals to one another. Dr. Michael Gazzaniga tested how the brain processes words it reads. He scanned a volunteer, who read words only in their left field of vision. The information was seen as an electrical current moving first from the right hemisphere, through the corpus callosum to the left hemisphere, where it was processed.

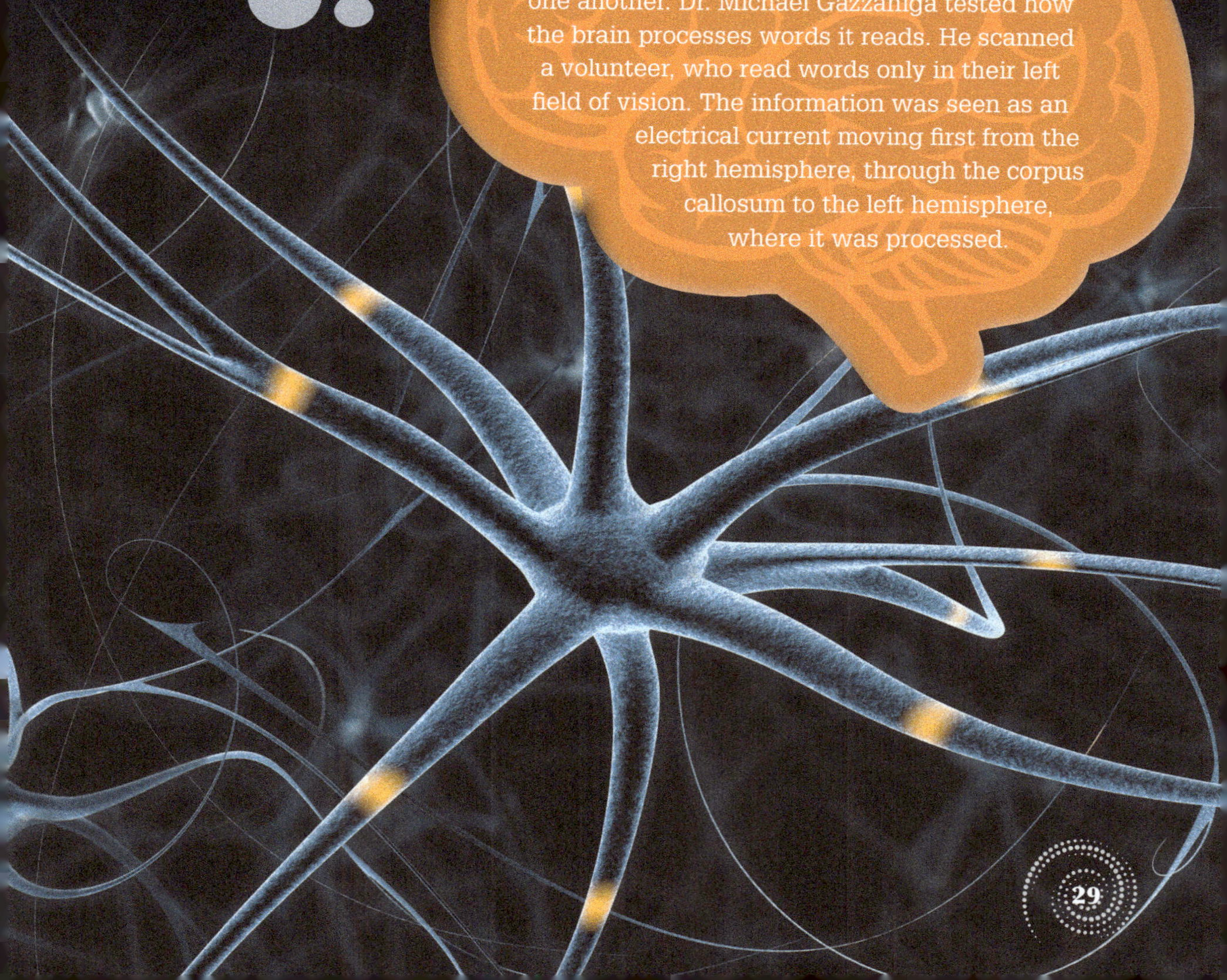

Split Personalities?

Alien hand syndrome, and the experiences of Vicky and Paul S, may make us wonder if splitting the brain can cause split personalities. If the left-hemisphere person who speaks does not know why his right hemisphere is drawing the picture of an elephant, is there one person in the brain, or two?

The studies of split-brain patients showed that most of those who recovered from their surgery recovered their ability to coordinate their bodies. All of them saw themselves as one individual. Dr. Michael Gazzaniga theorized that the two sides of the brain adjusted and that the more rational left hemisphere came up with reasonable explanations to explain away any strangeness. For example, a patient was shown the word "face" to his left hemisphere, and the word "smile" to the right hemisphere. The right hand drew a face with a smile. When the patient was asked why the face was smiling, he hastily answered, "Who wants a sad face around?" The right hemisphere can still perform tasks asked specifically of it, but the left hemisphere of these patients seems to accept this, and build explanations that help make sense of what happened. Similarly, Vicky learned to get her hands to work with each other. Even when the brain is divided, it seems to find ways to adapt.

Do split-brained patients also have split personalities, or do the two sides of the brain learn to accommodate each other?

Which is worse to put in your boss's coffee—rat poison or sugar? Both sides of the brain are involved in moral decisions!

INSIDE YOUR BRAIN

What role do both sides of the brain perform in moral decisions? In a 2009 study, scientists told stories to split-brain patients and asked their opinions. Since this was all done through spoken language, it was the left brain of the patients that heard and answered. One story told of someone who wanted to poison their boss by putting rat poison in their coffee but failed because they mistakenly used sugar. The other story told of someone who accidentally killed their boss by thinking the rat poison they were mixing into the coffee was sugar. Most people would judge that the person in the first story is a bad person while the other person is not, but the split-brain patients reasoned that both scenarios were morally the same. This suggests that both sides of the brain contribute to making moral decisions. However, friends of split-brain patients notice nothing bad about the moral decisions these patients make.

CHAPTER 5

WHY IS OUR BRAIN DIVIDED?

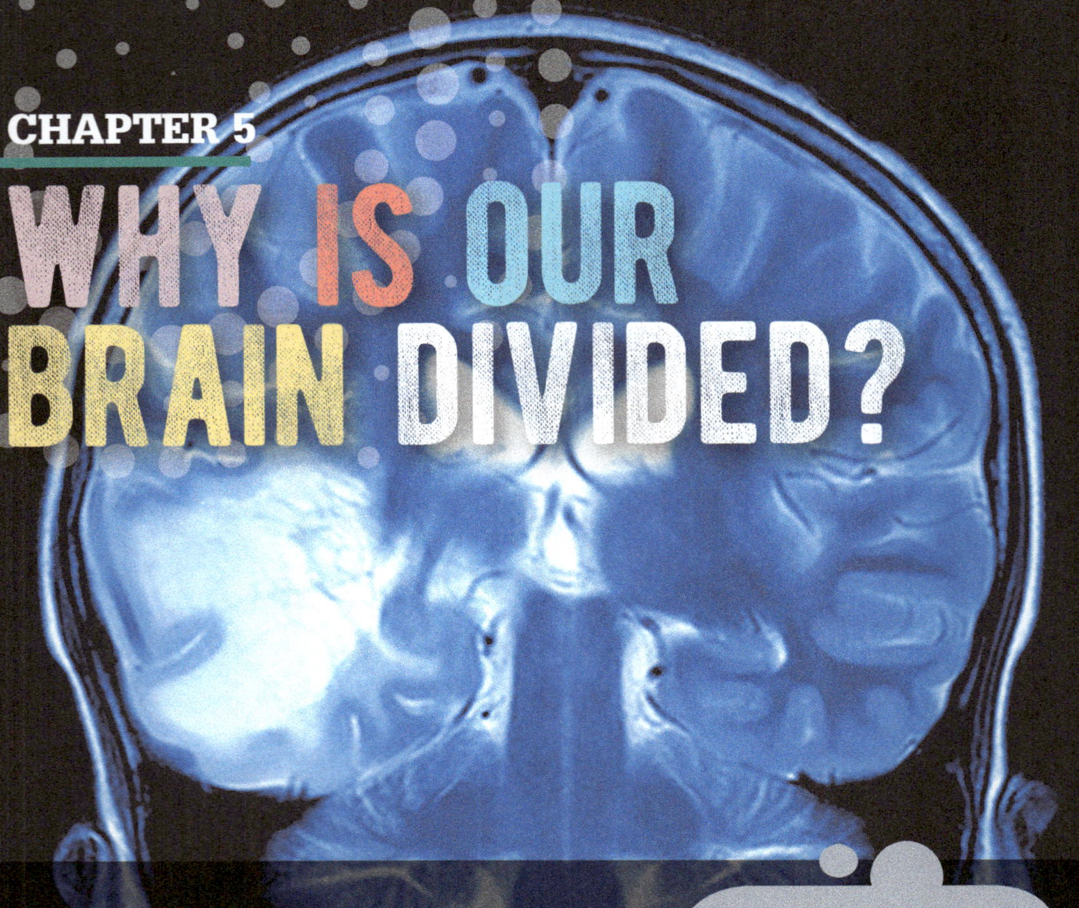

Despite the fact that both hemispheres of our brain work together as a unit, our brains must have evolved to have two hemispheres for a reason. There is usually a good reason why every other part of our body is the way it is. So why do we have two hemispheres? Neurologists are still exploring possible answers.

The Yakovlevian torque, or lopsided brain, may have evolved as speech became more important to our species.

As we have already learned, the hemispheres are not symmetrical in humans. The left hemisphere is broader at the back, while the right hemisphere is broader at the front. The twentieth-century neuroanatomist Dr. Paul Ivan Yakovlev described it as being as if somebody had taken the brain and twisted, or torqued, it slightly. As a result, this feature has been called the Yakovlevian torque.

Babies need well-developed right hemispheres for facial recognition and processing emotions.

Baby Survival

Further studies suggested this "torque" might be related to how the brain continues to develop and grow from birth until we are adults. In fact, the brain quadruples in size in the preschool years alone. The brain cannot put all its effort into growing and into building synapses in all areas at once—it is more efficient to concentrate development on where it is most needed. The right hemisphere grows faster in the first year after babies are born, before the left hemisphere catches up. The right hemisphere is in charge of recognizing faces, experiencing and processing emotions, and intuition. These are all key skills in a baby as it bonds with its caregivers and tries to ensure its immediate needs are met. Through this first year, it is possible the left hemisphere is holding back until the baby has built these core skills, at which point it is ready to learn how to speak. As we know, the left hemisphere is the location of the language control center.

INSIDE YOUR BRAIN

There are four stages in a child's cognitive development. From birth to two years of age, most babies learn about the world through their senses, by touching, smelling, looking, and listening. Between ages two and seven, children develop imagination and memory. They can understand how some things symbolize other things as well as concepts like the past and future. From ages seven through eleven, they begin to understand that the world does not revolve around them, and that they exist with other individuals who may think or act differently than they do. Finally, from age eleven, children understand logic, solve problems, and plan for the future. These stages align with how the lobes and hemispheres of the brain grow and develop.

The common toad's right hemisphere is on the lookout for danger, while the left side hunts for prey.

Answers in Animals

We know that most animals have brain hemispheres. The more evolved or complex the animal, the more prominent the hemispheres tend to be. Reptiles, birds, and mammals all have hemispheres, but the hemispheres are less developed in amphibians and fish. Scientists have studied how animals react to threats and food seen on their left side and on their right side, revealing some interesting facts about the uses of the left and right hemispheres. In studies, amphibian species like the common toad react differently to threats and food viewed on their left side than on their right. The toads were more likely to strike at prey if it was seen in the right field of vision, which is processed by the left hemisphere. Yet the toads reacted far more quickly to jump away from threats that were coming from their left side, processed by their right brains.

Neurologists studying the brains of animals such as dogs and birds have noticed that the left side of the brain is more often used when attention must be narrowly focused. For instance, a bird that is pecking at seeds on the ground has to be able to tell whether what it is pecking at is a seed or a pebble. While it is focused on the task at hand, its left hemisphere is very active. When animals know something is important and want to be precise about it, they use the left hemisphere of their brain. The same is true of humans!

All About Focus

Through his research, Dr. Roger Sperry argued that the left hemisphere of the brain was connected to linear thinking (thinking from A to B), logic, and facts, while the right hemisphere was connected with holistic thinking (thinking about the whole issue), intuition, understanding body language, and emotions. There is evidence to suggest that the fact that the left and right sides of the brain look at the world differently is an important survival trait for the human race. The question comes down to focus and connecting with the world.

When we are focusing on something specific, or figuring out a strategy, we are heavily using our left brains. Yet, at the same time, the right side of the brain remains broadly vigilant, keeping an eye out for threats or friends, and other unexpected events that we may have to deal with. The left side of our brain showed our early selves where the fruits were and how to pick them, while the right side of the brain stayed on the lookout for jaguars. To do this most effectively, we needed the two sides of the brain to specialize in their different areas of expertise, but to be able to work together.

SPEAK YOUR MIND

Most modern humans are unlikely to encounter jaguars in their neighborhood. But can you think of examples where broad awareness of your environment is important to you today? Can you think of times when you have used your intuitive awareness of a threat to keep yourself safe? Give reasons for your answers.

Hopefully, our right brains are on the lookout for traffic, even if our left brains are focusing on homework.

Even a tiny kitten can have intense focus, provided by its left brain, but it tends to show less empathy than a human!

Bigger Human Hemispheres

The combination of narrow focus and general alertness is where the two large but well-connected hemispheres of our brain start to separate humans from other animals. We have much more developed hemispheres than other animals, and this may be part of what makes us a highly adaptable and intelligent species. Remember that the parietal, occipital, and temporal lobes deal with taking in and reacting to the sights and sounds and other signals of the world around us. On the other hand, the frontal lobe is for reasoning, reacting with emotion, solving problems, and planning. The frontal lobe's job is sometimes to put a pause on the other three lobes, so that we can step back and think instead of just reacting with an impulse. This is part of what makes us different from dogs or common toads. And how we react is influenced by how the hemispheres work together.

Building Civilizations

The way our very specialized but closely linked hemispheres work together has allowed us not just to survive (finding fruit and escaping those jaguars), but also to build civilizations. A key fact is that our brains allow us to understand other individuals, see their point of view, and possibly cooperate with them. The human species can interact with the world and use it (left-hemisphere traits), but also imagine possible new cities, cooperate with one another to sail across the ocean to discover new lands, and write literature filled with implicit meanings and metaphor (right-hemisphere traits).

The fact that the left and right hemispheres share their different strengths gives us huge advantages as a species. The left hemisphere allows us to focus in on the important details and make decisions. The right hemisphere allows us to see beyond the moment and beyond our own needs as an individual. If you cannot consider the possibilities of the future, you just fight for the present, and if you cannot see the details, you cannot make good decisions. Both of these sets of skills are important in making good long-term decisions and are the basis of how we all get along and work together in society.

SPEAK YOUR MIND

How easy do you find it to introduce yourself to somebody new? What do you feel are the reasons for your response? How important is your imagination and intuition in deciding whether to make friends with someone, or to stay away? Give reasons for your answers.

Unlike most other species, humans are capable of cooperating with complete strangers.

CHAPTER 6

BRINGING IT ALL TOGETHER

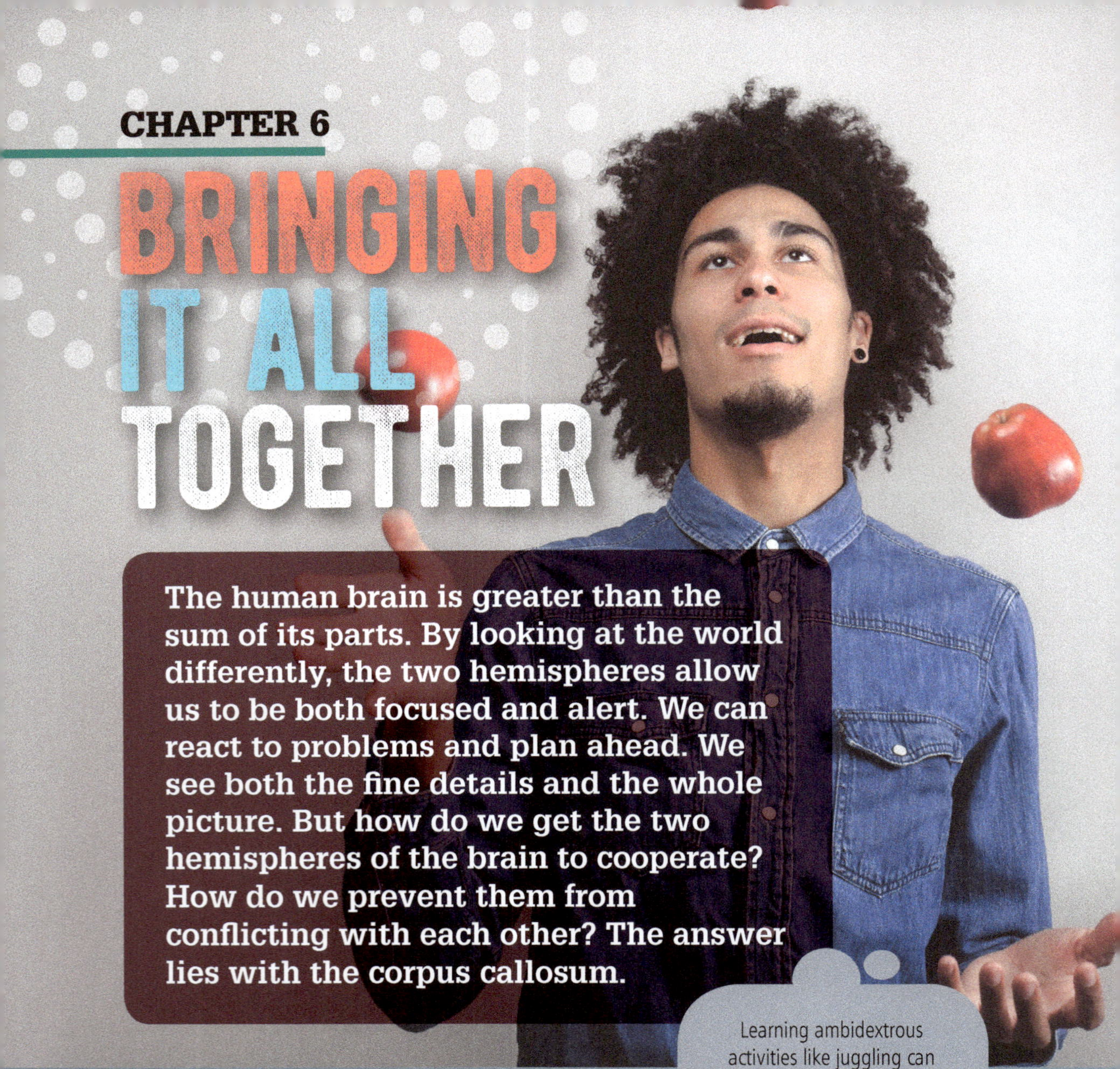

The human brain is greater than the sum of its parts. By looking at the world differently, the two hemispheres allow us to be both focused and alert. We can react to problems and plan ahead. We see both the fine details and the whole picture. But how do we get the two hemispheres of the brain to cooperate? How do we prevent them from conflicting with each other? The answer lies with the corpus callosum.

Learning ambidextrous activities like juggling can increase the size of the corpus callosum linking the two hemispheres.

The corpus callosum is itself divided into four parts, called the rostrum, genu, body, and splenium. The rostrum and genu connect the frontal lobes of the left and right hemispheres, while the body and splenium connect the temporal and occipital lobes. This means that the body and splenium of the corpus callosum are coordinating what the left and right ear hear, and what is seen in the left and right fields of vision. This is important because we use both ears to locate sounds, and we need

Each nerve fiber, also called an axon, is surrounded by a myelin sheath, which acts like a plastic coating around an electrical wire.

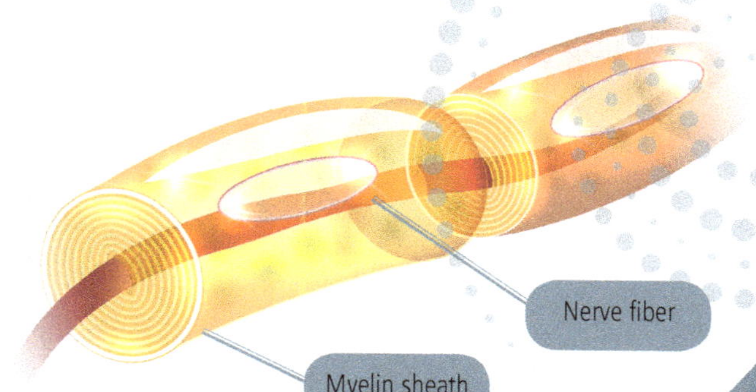

to coordinate vision from both sides to understand our surroundings. The splenium also connects the parietal lobes of the brain, which allows the two lobes to work together to locate where something has touched us. While certain brain functions are under the control of a particular hemisphere, the other hemisphere always has a role to play. The left hemisphere understands words, but the right hemisphere understands metaphor and context. And between them, the corpus callosum provides the only link.

White Matter

The corpus callosum is made of "white matter," whereas much of the brain is "gray matter." Gray matter is mostly cells called neurons, while white matter is nerve fibers. These fibers are perfectly structured to transfer the electrical signals sent out by the neurons. This shows that the corpus callosum is a conduit to send signals back and forth between the hemispheres. We have already learned about what happens to the brain if the corpus callosum is severed. Yet the corpus callosum is more than just a connection between the two hemispheres—it manages the signals that pass back and forth between the hemispheres, like a traffic cop.

INSIDE YOUR BRAIN

Left-handed people are fairly rare, but people who are naturally ambidextrous are rarer still. Only 1 percent of the population can use their right and left hands equally well. Many people who call themselves ambidextrous are actually left-handed but trained themselves to do tasks with their right hand. Similarly, right-handers can become ambidextrous if they injure their right arm. There are also activities that encourage great skill in both hands, including typing, martial arts, and surgery.

The corpus callosum acts like a traffic cop, keeping the transfer of information manageable.

The Traffic Cop?

The corpus callosum was not identified as a part of the brain until 1908. Neurologists began to understand its function only in the late 1950s. Its use is not fully understood to this day. One theory is that it exists not just to connect the two hemispheres of the brain, but to cut communications between them when necessary.

Why would this be important? In an emergency, your body goes into a fight or flight response. It has to react quickly to a situation and decide whether to run or whether to defend itself. It needs information fast, and it cannot be bogged down by unimportant details. In this case, the corpus callosum restricts the traffic between the frontal lobes and lets the more automatic brain stem and cerebellum respond.

No Leakage

A related theory suggests the corpus callosum enforces the dominance of one hemisphere over the other. Scientists point to "mirror movements" as evidence to back this theory up. In young children whose corpus callosum is not fully developed, and in older adults where the corpus callosum is thinning out, the voluntary (deliberate) movement of one hand is sometimes mirrored by the involuntary (not deliberate) movement of the other. It is as if the thoughts of one hemisphere, controlling one hand, are leaking over to the other side. This would suggest that the corpus callosum is essential for preventing this leakage, so it must sometimes prevent the passing of brainwaves from one hemisphere to the other. However, this theory is still being debated by neurologists, and is not accepted by everyone.

SPEAK YOUR MIND

The corpus callosum is reported to be larger in musicians than nonmusicians. People who are left-handed and ambidextrous also have a corpus callosum that may be up to 11 percent larger than right-handed people. Why might musicians have a more developed organ for coordinating the two hemispheres of the brain? What other ways can you think of to exercise your corpus callosum? Give reasons for your answers.

Learning music early, while the brain is still developing, may help increase the size of the corpus callosum.

Popular Psychology

Neurologists understand that, while there are differences between the hemispheres of the brain and how they work, the differences are not as clear cut as logic versus emotion, rationality versus creativity, or numbers versus music. The old theories about the left and right hemispheres of the brain are taught mostly to show how neurology's understanding of the brain has changed.

That has not stopped the idea of left brain and right brain taking root in popular culture. People who are seen as more analytical or good at math are said to be "left-brained." People suggest that music education is good for the "right brain" even though both hands are needed to play instruments. You see references to these outdated theories in self-help books and online quizzes.

Helping Out

While this overgeneralized view of the hemispheres is not where neurology is or where it is going, it can be helpful in starting our understanding of the brain. It shows that there are differences in different brains that should be explored. You could also consider using the different ways your hemispheres view the world to help you when you have problems or when you are learning in school. For example, if you have difficulty understanding instructions people say to you, consider that processing something audibly is a left-hemisphere characteristic. You could try working with your right hemisphere by writing the instructions down.

There is nothing wrong with taking Internet quizzes to tell whether you are more "left-brained" or "right-brained." These quizzes encourage you to think about how you think. Just take the results with a grain of salt. Neurologists do!

People who learn better by listening are more often left-brain dominant.

People who learn better through visuals or movement are more often right-brain dominant.

INSIDE YOUR BRAIN

Over the years, various teachers and psychologists have put forward the idea of different "learning styles," or the idea that different people learn best through different means of teaching. These learning styles are not agreed on by most scientists, who do not think they adequately describe the many ways that children and adults learn. Commonly discussed "learning styles" include visual learning, in which learners prefer to see information through words, pictures, and symbols; auditory learning, in which learners prefer to hear information; and kinesthetic learning, in which learners prefer to experience new ideas through moving, touching, and doing.

AMAZING HEMISPHERES

The division of our brain into well-developed left and right hemispheres appears to be a vital feature of our highly successful species. The tasks done by each hemisphere not only give us good survival skills, but may explain how we see one another as individuals and how we work together, helping us flourish as a species.

Neurology has developed immensely over the past two centuries. Thanks to technologies such as MRI and PET scanners, neurologists no longer have to look at the brains of the dead, or at

The first gamma "knife" surgery took place in 1991.

patients who are having surgery. They can see how the brains of healthy people work, what parts of the brain respond to different tasks, and how the parts of the brain communicate with one another.

New Technology

The brain remains a tantalizing mystery for scientists, but neurology is a developing field. Technologies continue to improve, and scientists continue to do research. MEG scanners are getting more precise, painting more detailed pictures of our brains. New tools like the gamma "knife," which is not really a knife at all, use focused beams of radiation to allow doctors to make tiny incisions—just the size of single cells—in the brain. With this technology, brain surgeons can fix problems without opening up the skull.

New Answers

As our understanding of the brain grew, we thought we knew all that we needed to know about how it worked. However, the mid-twentieth century understanding of the hemispheres as divided between reason and emotion turned out to be inaccurate. Our ideas are almost constantly changing because scientists continue to ask questions and test assumptions. It is likely that some of what we think we know about the brain today may turn out to be wrong. Luckily, some of our best brains are working toward discovering new answers.

SPEAK YOUR MIND

Scientists are getting closer to duplicating the functions of a brain using computers. Computers can already process facts and numbers far faster than human minds. One day, could microscopic computers enhance our brains? Could we hook up our left hemisphere to a computer but find we still need a human right hemisphere to do a range of other tasks? Give reasons for your answers.

Computers are already interfacing with brains. For example, scientists have used sensors to try to restore the sight of blind patients.

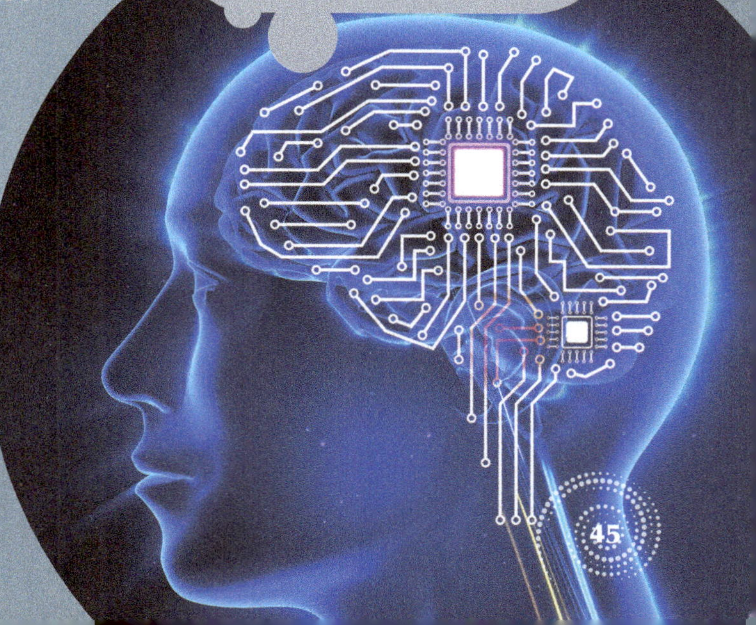

GLOSSARY

aphasia An inability to understand speech or to speak.

autopsy An examination of a body after death.

brain stem The part of the base of the brain that controls our heartbeat and breathing.

cerebellum The area at the back of the brain that controls the working of our muscles.

cerebral cortex The part of the brain where conscious thought takes place.

cognitive The ability to gain knowledge through thought, experience, and the senses.

corpus callosum A link between the left and right hemispheres.

depression A condition in which a person suffers from a low mood over a long period.

epilepsy A disorder that can cause people to become unconscious and to have uncontrolled movements of the body.

genetic Relating to genes, which are the building blocks of all cells and determine what the cells do.

hemispheres Halves of a sphere; the two halves of the brain.

lateralization The division of brain functions between one hemisphere and the other.

lobe A curved or rounded part of something. Each hemisphere of the brain is divided into four lobes: frontal, parietal, occipital, and temporal.

magnetic resonance imaging (MRI) scan A process in which a machine takes detailed pictures of the inside of the body.

magnetoencephalography (MEG) scanner A machine that scans electrical currents that pass through the brain.

neuroanatomist A doctor who closely studies the parts of the brain and nervous system.

neurologists Doctors who study the brain and treat the problems that can occur.

neurons Nerve cells in the brain.

neuroscience The study of the brain and nervous system.

positron emission tomography (PET) scan A process in which a machine scans the brain to see which parts are working.

seizure A sudden attack in which the body moves in an uncontrolled and violent way

stroke Damage to the brain caused by the sudden loss of blood to a portion of the brain.

FOR MORE INFORMATION

Books

Abramovitz, Melissa. *Brain Science*. Minneapolis, MN: Essential Library, 2016.

Meister, Cari. *Totally Wacky Facts About the Mind*. North Mankato, MN: Capstone Press, 2016.

Potts, Francesca. *Left Brain, Right Brain: Facts, Trivia, and Quizzes*. Minneapolis, MN: Lerner Publications, 2018.

Szpirglas, Jeff, and Danielle Saint-Onge. *Your Changing Brain: A Guidebook*. New York, NY: Crabtree Publishing Company, 2018.

Websites

Discover the different parts of the brain at:
ducksters.com/science/brain.php

Find out all about your amazing brain at:
easyscienceforkids.com/all-about-your-amazing-brain

Learn about neuroscience through experiments, articles, and games at:
faculty.washington.edu/chudler/neurok.html

Read interesting facts about the brain from National Geographic Kids at:
kids.nationalgeographic.com/explore/science/your-amazing-brain

INDEX